Ethical Capitalism

ETHICAL CAPITALISM

A Proposal for a Better World

SEBASTIEN MOUTON

www.ethicap.org

Ethical Capitalism: A Proposal for a Better World

Copyright © 2023 Sebastien Mouton

Cover art copyright © 2023 Sebastien Mouton

Cover design concept, editing and formatting
by Sebastien Mouton

First edition: June 2023

ISBN: 978-2-9588225-1-4

I would like to express my gratitude to Allister Heath, Derek Anderson, Daniel Tierney and Jacob Becker for their insights and feedback.

CONTENTS

To Aude, who gave me so much love
I had to try and share some of it.

INTRODUCTION

Capitalism has been responsible for the most extraordinary increase in standard of living in the history of humanity[1]. We transitioned from toiling relentlessly for basic survival to enjoying more free time, luxurious food, and sophisticated entertainment than could ever be thought possible.

Democracy has led to the highest drop in inequality in history. We went from the nobility having the right of life and death over starving peasants to the concept of middle class.

But our system is broken. While it was able to get us out of straw houses, our antiquated model leaves behind too many people, provides very little return on debilitating levels of taxation, does not represent our interests and

---

[1] Cynthia Taft Morris, How Fast and Why Did Early Capitalism Benefit the Majority? (1995)

opinions well, and has proven itself unable to solve modern challenges.

Capitalism has turned to a predatory form, where there is too little correlation between individual reward and the Common Good. The individual pursuit of wealth is not increasing common well-being anymore. Too many of the sharpest minds are turning to the highest-paying endeavors, with little positive externality. Compounded by rising inequalities[2], this has led to increased resentment and class warfare that will only get worse if we do not alter our current trajectory.

Democracy is in crisis. The level of discontent is so high[3] that many people in the Western World have begun to relativize the actions and models of dictatorships across the globe. The unhappiness in the wealthiest parts of the world is so strong that countries employing systematic persecutions, totalitarianism, and even genocides do not necessarily appear to have a drastically inferior governance system[4].

---

[2] Gabriel Zucman, Annual Reviews (2019), Global Wealth Inequality

[3] Lee Rainie, Andrew Perrin, Pew Research Center (2019), Key findings about Americans' declining trust in government and each other

[4] Sarah Repucci and Amy Slipowitz, Freedom House (2022), The Global Expansion of Authoritarian Rule

This problem is so dire, so critical to the future of our civilization, that none of us can shy away from it[5]. If we do not change course very soon, our way of life is at serious risk of being annihilated by climate change, artificial intelligence, social upheaval or authoritarianism.

Our ruling elites have ignored the issue for decades. Not because they did not care, but because they had no idea how to solve it. The electorate, which does not dwell on the causes of the predicament, is so fed up that they started to elect whoever promised the most different path. And because none of our politicians had any clue, they did not offer any significant solution. That is of course an environment where demagogues shine. The Western World started to elect populists who also had no clue how to solve the problems, but were happy to promulgate simplistic ideas to get elected and obtain personal power.

This is why I am proposing a new socioeconomic model, which builds on capitalism by incorporating the notion of Common Good at its core, and enhances our political system by adding direct democracy.

This new model addresses what I consider to be both the most important and most overlooked problem of our world: the lack of alignment between individual effort and collective benefit. The current system enables individuals

---

[5] Jonathan Perry, United Nations (2021), Trust in public institutions: Trends and implications for economic security

and companies to enrich themselves through economic activities that have no benefit to society. It is disturbing to realize that we are the most clever, most numerous on earth we have ever been, and yet we are unable to solve our current challenges. This is not due to lack of work, as we are the most productive we have ever been. This is not due to extreme selfishness, as humans are no more self-centered as they have ever been. This issue arises from misalignment: the Common Good is simply completely absent from the parameters of our system, and it is foolishness to expect individuals to independently act towards the global optimum.

My proposal fixes this alignment issue by creating a correlation between individual profits and the Common Good. It keeps all of the openness and motivation of the free enterprise principles of capitalism, while adding this crucial element.

This model transcends the perennial left-right debate by harmoniously combining efficiency and humanity without compromise. This change is revolutionary in concept yet evolutionary in its implementation, both transformational enough to tackle these severe issues, and practical enough for real-world application. It is rooted in both solid economic principles and fundamental human psychology.

We will embark on a journey together to discuss the importance of power systems (Part 0), the origins of our current system (Part 1), and its flaws (Part 2). We will discuss fundamental principles for dreaming a better model (Part 3), then I will detail a specific paradigm that gathers all this insight into a proposal for a better socioeconomic model (Part 4). We will list some arguments for it (Part 5) and discuss its implementation in the real world (Part 6).

0

THE CRITICAL IMPORTANCE OF POWER SYSTEMS

"The price good men pay for indifference to public affairs is to be ruled by evil men." -Plato

Before we dive deeply into the problems with our current system and discuss the solution, I want to try and convince you that this work is worth doing by emphasizing the importance of our organizational system in everything we do.

Focus on the System, Not on the Individuals

Human societies are governed by complex rules that we call our socioeconomic system. The political and economic aspects, democracy and capitalism in the Free World, are its two fundamental pillars.

We tend to focus on individuals, but we need to focus more on the system. It is not as natural, as our brain is wired to react to other humans, but it is crucial. The general consensus is that politicians of all sides are incompetent and corrupt. Are all humans like that? No. So clearly, we have a system that selects for this type of person, and we need to change that.

But this negative selection bias might also conceal a tendency to oversimplify problems others must solve. The idea that people in charge are malicious and stupid is easy to hold, until we are responsible for a large project. Then it suddenly becomes clear how challenging it is to manage all stakeholders, and how we are cornered into making suboptimal decisions. The real world is just hard and messy.

While systems were initially built to fit around one individual (typically a king or emperor), it got out of hand, and the situation has reversed: people in power now fit into the system. Conspiracy theories often assign blame to individual people because that makes so much more sense to our primal brain, but that is simply not true. Everyone, even Jeff Bezos and Bill Gates, is a little lost in our world, and none of us fully understands it. It is similar to the way we all rely on computers everyday, even though no single individual can fully grasp all of their components. We build and build on top of each other's work until we do not understand anything anymore.

On the Self-Centeredness of Humans

It is all the more important to focus on the system that the alternative is doomed to fail. Indeed, current movements tend to try to change society by shaming people in power into doing what is right. This not only holds little hope, but it is also hypocritical. All humans, poor or wealthy, look at their own interests first. Several distinct theories establish that point.

According to evolutionary theory, humans have evolved to be self-centered as a survival mechanism. In early human history, individuals who were more focused on their own needs and desires were more likely to survive and reproduce than those who were not.[6]

Freud's theory suggests that the ego, the part of the psyche responsible for mediating between the demands of the id (the primitive and instinctual part of the psyche) and the demands of the external world, has a natural tendency to prioritize the individual's own needs and desires.[7]

Social identity theory posits that people tend to identify with certain groups, such as their nationality, religion, or social class, and that this identification leads them to view

---

[6] David Buss, Evolutionary Psychology, The new science of the mind (2015)

[7] Sigmund Freud, The Ego and the Id (1923)

members of their own group more positively and members of other groups more negatively.[8]

Finally, there are a number of cognitive biases that can contribute to self-centeredness, such as the self-serving bias (the tendency to attribute positive outcomes to one's own abilities and negative outcomes to external factors) and the fundamental attribution error (the tendency to over-emphasize dispositional factors when explaining other people's behavior)[9].

This self-centeredness is a critical psychological aspect to take into account when devising a human system. This is not to say that we are incapable of caring for others. On the contrary, altruism is also a fundamental human trait. But in what manner do we express that characteristic?

Kin selection theory suggests that humans are more likely to be altruistic towards close relatives, such as siblings, parents, and offspring, because helping them increases the likelihood of passing on shared genes.

---

[8] Krueger, J. I., & Funder, D. C., Towards a balanced social psychology: Causes, consequences, and cures for the problem-seeking approach to social behavior and cognition. Behavioral and Brain Sciences (2004), 27(3), 313-327.

[9] Ross, L., The intuitive psychologist and his shortcomings: Distortions in the attribution process. In L. Berkowitz (Ed.), Advances in experimental social psychology (1977) (Vol. 10, pp. 173-220). Academic Press.

Reciprocal altruism theory proposes that humans can be altruistic towards non-relatives if they expect to receive a benefit in return, either immediately or in the future.

Reputation management theory suggests that humans may engage in altruistic behavior in order to enhance their own social reputation and gain benefits such as increased status, trust, and cooperation from others.

Finally, group selection theory proposes that humans may be altruistic towards members of their own group or community, even at a cost to themselves, because this behavior can increase the group's overall fitness and survival.

So only the group selection theory could justify the current mechanism of our society to rely on individuals to do what is right, instead of having a stronger system. Unfortunately, though once a favored notion, group selection theory was cast aside by evolutionary biologists following George Williams' criticism[10]. However, this was not because group selection was implausible, as Williams himself argued that it could occur in certain species like honeybees. Rather, the issue lay in the rarity of circumstances that could make group selection probable, such as the collective destiny of group members, minimal reproductive rivalry within the group, and repeated instances of

---

[10] George Christopher Williams, Princeton Science Library (1966), Adaptation and Natural Selection: A Critique of Some Current Evolutionary Thought

group reproduction and extinction. Given the scarcity of such circumstances in nature, group selection was deemed unlikely to have had a substantial impact on most species, and particularly in humans.

The Legitimacy of Power

Let us briefly discuss history from an unusual angle: how ruling powers justified their legitimacy.

For millennia, institutions of power claimed legitimacy through religion and nationalism. Kings were appointed directly by God. Priests served as locally dispatched guardians of individual behavior. Men were called by their God to wage war and send to His judgment those who did not pray in the correct fashion. But the religious justification has faded away. In the USA, where many early immigrants fled religious persecution in England, France, and Germany, the First Amendment of the Constitution established the separation of church and state in 1791. In France, la *Loi concernant la séparation des Eglises et de l'Etat* was adopted in 1905.

As religious arguments weakened, nationalism became the primary legitimizer for governing institutions. And indeed, the countless wars of the 19th and first half of the 20th century left little room for challenging that ideology. But the Western World focused on international peace after the trauma of the two world wars, resulting in an unprecedented era of peace.

This amazing achievement left a void for governing bodies. Devoid of the inarguable legitimacy provided by religion or active warfare, reigning powers began to be judged on their economic output from the mid-1900s. The main debate, to put it politely, was between capitalism and communism. The Communist East and Capitalist West waged an ideological war throughout the second half of the 20th century. Capitalism has comprehensively won the argument. While most countries in the world now operate under a capitalist system[11], only five countries in the world declare themselves to be communist[12]: China, Cuba, Laos, Vietnam and North Korea. And China, the most economically successful among them, actually operates under an economic model much closer to capitalism than communism, having embraced a market economy and private entrepreneurship. Karl Marx would not be proud.

The Importance of Alignment

When it comes to making progress in a complex system, like our socioeconomic system, alignment is the key element, although it is often overlooked. By alignment, I mean ensuring that the efforts made are all moving us,

---

[11] World Population Review, Capitalist Countries 2023

[12] World Population Review, Communist Countries 2023

however slightly, towards the end goal. In real life, these end goals are often fuzzy and poorly defined, leading us to replace them by a measurable target, and focus on making large strides in that direction. Yet, in many cases, smaller improvements, more aligned with our end goal, are what wins in the long term.

This is exemplified by the development of ChatGPT from OpenAI, the large language model that has revolutionized the field of natural language processing. Contrary to popular belief, ChatGPT did not deeply improve its mathematical model or change the architecture of its neural network; rather, it implemented RLHF (reinforcement learning from human feedback), a method to align the effort more closely with the goal.

In traditional Reinforcement Learning, the decision-making agent receives rewards or punishments from its environment to learn which actions to take to maximize its net score. In RLHF, the agent receives feedback from a human observer. This person provides information about the quality of the agent's actions, allowing the machine to learn more quickly and effectively than it would through trial-and-error alone.

1

THE ORIGINS OF THE CURRENT SYSTEM

Our current system has deep flaws that urgently need fixing. But before diving into them in the next section of this book, I want to take a brief moment to reflect on how we got here, and recognize how brilliant of an improvement it was, compared to anything that existed before.

Our Economic System

Capitalism

"Individual ambition serves the Common Good." -Adam Smith

Adam Smith, the father of modern economics, was quite the interesting character. Not only did he have a brilliant mind, he was also a lover of literature and a bit of a foodie. He had a particular weakness for oysters, which he would often consume in large quantities while pondering his economic theories. When he was not indulging in seafood, Smith could be found with his nose buried in a book.

Despite his love for oysters and literature, Adam Smith is best known for his pioneering work in the field of economics, which ultimately led to the invention of capitalism. He began writing his seminal work, The Wealth of Nations, in France in 1774, where he was hired by Chancellor of the Exchequer, Charles Townshend, to tutor his stepson, the Duke of Buccleuch. Despite the substantial sum of around £300 per year plus expenses, along with a £300 annual pension, Smith found little intellectual stimulation in Toulouse and its environs. His experiences changed dramatically when he traveled to Geneva and had the opportunity to meet with the renowned philosopher Voltaire. Later, during his stay in Paris, he became acquainted with the ideas of the economic school of Physiocrats, led by François Quesnay, which left a deep impression on him. These encounters played a pivotal role in shaping Smith's thinking and establishing the theoretical basis of modern economics.

In "The Wealth of Nations", Smith argued that the most efficient way to grow an economy was through free-market capitalism, where individuals and businesses are allowed to pursue their own self-interest without interference from the government. This idea, which he famously referred to as the "invisible hand", revolutionized the way we think about economics and has had a profound impact on the world as we know it today.

At the time, capitalism was a revolution. Its proponents saw in it the ultimate meritocracy that rewards the sharpest minds and hardest workers, the engine that drives innovation and progress, that turns ideas into reality and dreams into achievements.

They wanted a system where everyone has the opportunity to succeed, regardless of their background or status. No barriers to entry, no government regulations to stifle your creativity or ambition. The only thing that matters is how well you can compete in the marketplace. Companies are constantly vying for consumer dollars, they must constantly innovate and improve in order to stay ahead. This competition drives progress, spurs technological advancements, and fuels economic growth.

Capitalism has lifted billions of people out of poverty, generated a myriad of innovations, and created a level of prosperity that would have been unthinkable just a few centuries ago.

Decentralization

"The Whole is Greater than the Sum of its Parts" -Aristotle

The concept of capitalism is so important that it has been the subject of countless attempts at definition by economists. Allow me to submit my definition to you:

> Capitalism is the decentralization of economic decisions.

Notice that I am not focusing on capital or deregulation in this definition. All these important aspects of capitalism derive from the magic that happens when you simply move the decision-making from a central authority to individual agents.

Decentralization is counter-intuitively an amazingly powerful concept. So powerful that it is at the origin of life itself. Indeed, that is what physicists call *emergence*: the appearance of properties absent from individual parts, when interacting as a whole. Life *emerges* from lifeless individual atoms.

If you are not convinced yet, let me provide another example of how powerful decentralization is. Machine Learning is the technology that is revolutionizing the world as we speak. It is the mathematical domain behind

AI chatbots, financial trading, mortgage application, spam filtering, and chess playing. And what is the secret of Machine Learning? Yes, decentralization. We actually call it ensemble techniques.

The breakthrough was indeed to use many simple models (an *ensemble* of models), and then aggregate their outputs. Before that, the focus of mathematics (particularly statistics, which predates Machine Learning) was to create increasingly large models, using subtle and complex understanding of the problem. Machine Learning ripped apart this whole idea, and simply threw an enormous amount of dumb models at the problem. And when we aggregated their answers, we magically found that their collective answer was more accurate that the sophisticated individual models that took years to come out of brilliant mathematical minds.

The most famous ensemble technique is the Neural Network. Each neuron, a dumb mathematical model that performs basic arithmetic on a handful of numbers, is aggregated together to produce a coherent sentence, an accurate estimate, or a relevant decision. And I will let you guess whether I am talking about artificial or organic neural networks.

While each individual model might be simple, with very limited information, the aggregation technique should be well crafted. This has been the main research effort of

Machine Learning over the last few years: designing increasingly performant neural network architectures.

And that is what is broken in our society today. The problem is not that individual citizens are not informed well enough or not smart enough. It is that our aggregating function, the architecture of the network that translates the will of individuals into a collective decision, is thoroughly inefficient. And how could it be otherwise when we have not worked on it in so long?

Our Political System

Imagine ancient Athens, the birthplace of democracy. In the 5th century BCE, the Athenians were the first to introduce a system of government where every citizen had a say in the decisions that affected their lives. It was not perfect - women, slaves, and non-citizens were excluded from the political process - but it was a groundbreaking development in human history. And it worked surprisingly well. By debating and voting on issues, the Athenians were able to create a stable and prosperous society. They even defeated the mighty Persian Empire in battle, thanks in part to the unity and solidarity that democracy fostered.

Since then, democracy has spread around the world, and while each country has its own unique version of the system, the basic principles remain the same. This paradigm ensures that every voice is heard, and that no one group can dominate the others. Although not always easy, and despite numerous challenges associated with democratic governance, it has proven overall to be a remarkably effective way of organizing societies.

The United Nations Development Programme reports that democratic countries have higher rates of human development, including longer life expectancy, higher literacy rates, and greater access to basic healthcare and education[13].

The Corruption Perceptions Index, published by the coalition Transparency International, consistently finds that democratic countries have lower levels of corruption than non-democratic countries[14].

The Human Freedom Index, published by the Cato Institute, ranks countries based on their protection of civil liberties such as freedom of speech, religion, and assembly. The top-ranked countries are almost all democracies, while the least free countries are typically non-democratic[15].

These statistics suggest that democracy is not only a more fair and just system of government, but also one that leads

---

[13] United Nations, Human Development report 2022

[14] Transparency International, Corruption Perceptions Index 2022

[15] Cato Institute, Human Freedom Index 2023

to better economic, social, and political outcomes for its citizens.

2

THE PROBLEM WITH OUR SYSTEM

"Every nation gets the government it deserves." -Joseph de Maistre

The Problem

Capitalism and democracy were amazing inventions, but we have stopped meaningful improvements for too long, and our system is now obsolete and decadent.

Predatory Capitalism

Capitalism has turned to a predatory form that works against our collective interest. Individuals are opting in large numbers for economic activities that provide little to society, while maximizing[16] their own paycheck.

The anthropologist David Graeber argues[17] that almost half of our jobs are "bullshit jobs": "so completely pointless,

---

[16] Thomas Piketty, Capital in the Twenty First Century (2014)

[17] David Graeber, Bullshit Jobs (2018)

unnecessary, or pernicious that even the employee cannot justify its existence even though the employee feels obligated to pretend that this isn't the case."

Companies are driven by quarterly profits, and the horizon for the long-term view stops at the directors' planned departure date. Unfortunately, the average executive tenure has decreased to under 5 years and continues to trend downwards[18].

Inequalities are worsening for over 70% of the global population[19]. Thomas Piketty demonstrated in his seminal book "Capital in the Twenty-First Century" that increasing inequalities are a feature of our current form of capitalism, not an accident.

A specific issue for the Western World is the low income growth of the lower-income and middle class, squeezed between the rise in emerging countries and the "one per-cent". This is represented by the infamous Elephant Curve[20].

---

[18] PWC, CEO turnover at record high (2018)

[19] UNDESA, World Social Report 2020

[20] Lakner and Milanivic, Global Income Distribution: From the Fall of the Berlin Wall to the Great Recession (2013)

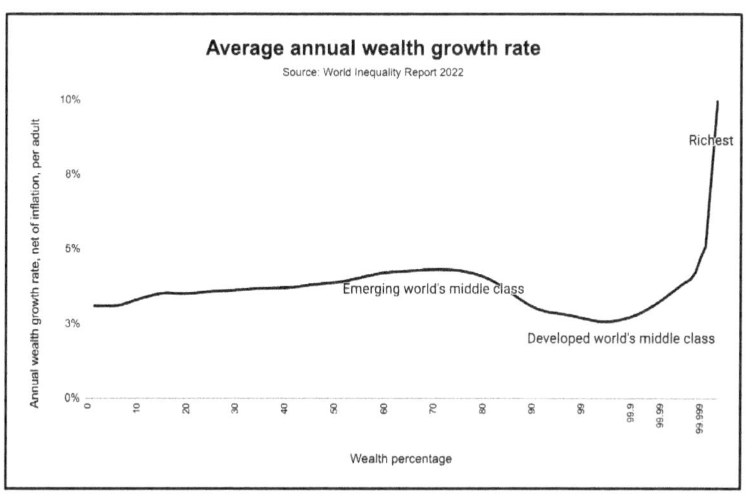

Taxation

For a large section of the political sphere, the answer to predatory capitalism lies in taxation. But governments are already taxing their citizens into oblivion. Let us look at average worldwide tax rates. When Bob, a good employee of WidgetCo generates $100 in profit for his company, the corporation pays 25% corporation tax[21]. That is $75 left. WidgetCo would not exist without its investors, but they need something because they do not like giving money for free, so it pays them 30% of what is left: $22.50.

But the government also taxes the dividend the investors receive, at a level of 30%. WidgetCo reinvests 20% ($15) of its profits in itself, to buy new machines and conduct R&D.

---

[21] Tax Foundation, Corporate Tax Rates Around the World 2022

The remaining $37.50 is for employees' compensation. And of course, the government taxes 30%[22] ($11.25) of that before it even reaches Bob's paycheck. Then Bob pays his 25% yearly income tax, so he receives net $19.69. And whenever he spends it, he pays 10% sales tax and feels happy not to pay the 21% VAT rate European countries charge[23].

Adding all of this, the average worldwide government effectively has a taxation rate slightly over 50%. The employee, the company, and the shareholders each receive about ⅙, while the government takes about half.

---

[22] Esteban Ortiz-Ospina and Max Roser, Our World in Data, Taxation

[23] Tax Foundation, 2022 VAT Rates in Europe

	Employee	Company	Shareholders	Government
Production	+ $100			
Corporation Tax				- $25
Dividend			- $15.75	
Dividend Tax				- $ 6.75
Reinvestment		-$15		
Employee Tax				- $ 11.25
Income Tax				- $ 6.56
Sales Tax				- $2
NET GAIN	$ 17.72	$ 15	$ 15.75	$ 51.53

This number is quite stunning. Moreover, this is a recent phenomenon. At the beginning of the 20th century, taxation levels, as a share of national income, were under 10%. It has multiplied fivefold in most western countries over the course of the century.

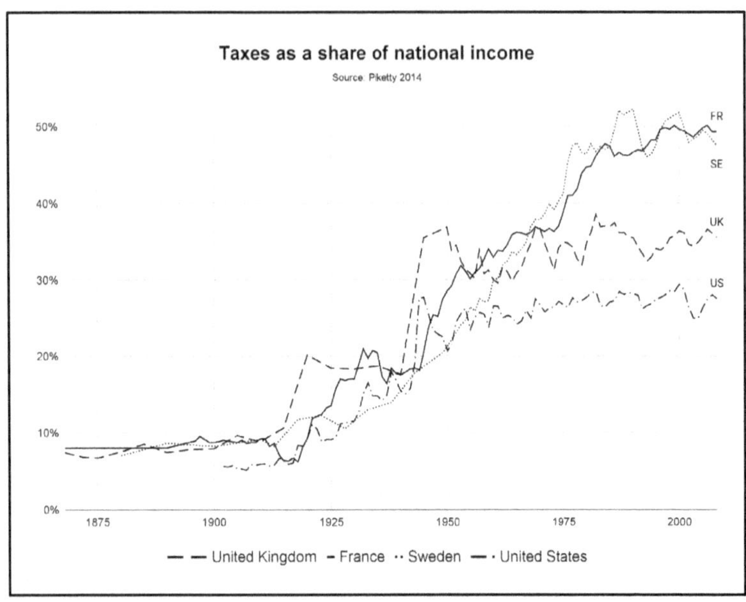

Crucially, citizens feel they get little in return for what is by far their biggest, though partially hidden, expense. Maybe the most striking example is France, which tops global rankings in terms of taxation, but where the dissatisfaction with public services is so high in recent years[24] that it also tops rankings on strikes[25].

---

[24] Faustine Carrié, Acteurs Publics, Baromètre des services publics

[25] Servet Yanatma, Euronews, Which countries have the most strikes in Europe

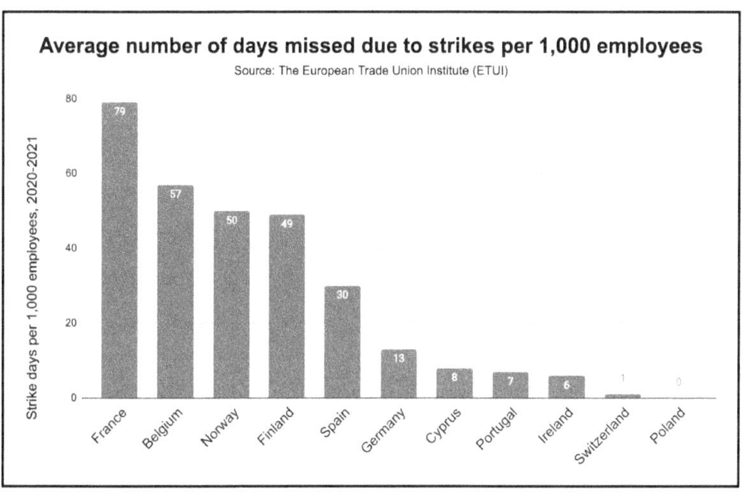

Loss of shared purpose

The distrust in our system, stemming from all these issues, has led to a disappearance of shared purpose. Humans have a fundamental need for meaning and a sense of belonging to a group. For millennia, these two philosophical necessities have been fulfilled largely by religions and nations. Whether you liked it or not, you were told in no uncertain terms where you belonged, and what your life's purpose was. Recent history has seen a decline in religious beliefs, leaving nations as the main bearers of that responsibility. But the collapse of trust in our system has broken this last bastion and left a void that people are scrambling to fill. This is why terrorism, extremist ideologies and populists are thriving[26]: we cannot abide a meaningless life.

This is also the reason behind the troubling trend we are currently witnessing: democracy is losing ground to authoritarianism, both in terms of the number of countries choosing one system over the other and in the shift of public opinion.

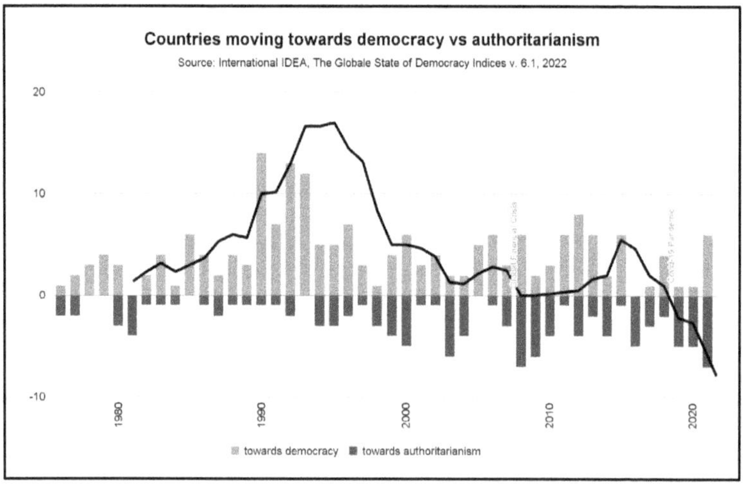

Note: this chart shows as positive values the number of countries moving towards democracy (from a hybrid or authoritarian regime to a democracy, or from an authoritarian to a hybrid regime), and shows as negative values the number of countries moving towards authoritarianism

---

[26] Séraphin Alava, Divina Frau-Meigs, Ghayda Hassan, UNESCO (2017), Youth and violent extremism on social media: mapping the research

(from democracy to a hybrid or authoritarian regime, or from a hybrid to an authoritarian regime).

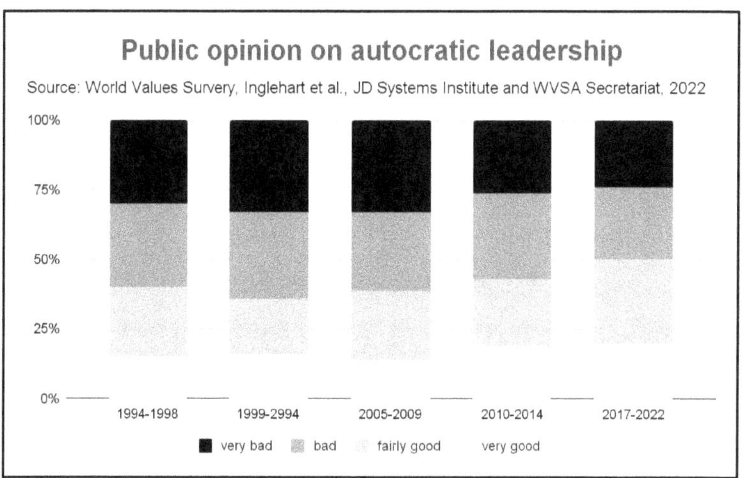

Note: the chart indicates the responses to the World Values Survey question: "Would you say that 'having a strong leader who does not have to bother with parliament and elections' is a very good, fairly good, fairly bad or very bad way of governing this country?"

The problem with our system is clear. But what solutions are proposed?

The Current Solutions

Let us briefly explore the mainstream solutions in the Western World. Summaries of this nature are necessarily a blunt instrument, so I will focus on the broad strokes rather than the nuances.

The Left's Approach

The Left tends to blame capitalism. Their solution is more regulation, more government.

Despite the rich capturing an increasing proportion of the nations' wealth[27], socialist rhetoric is failing to get a proper foothold. Why is the Left performing so poorly in an environment of increasing inequalities[28,29]? Because we have seen this movie before. We know from the examples of communist and extreme socialist countries around the world that this is not the answer. In addition, and very importantly, we distrust our governments. We know they are unable to utilize efficiently the enormous sums of money at their disposal. We have experienced too many times that more government destroys wealth, increases corruption[30] and takes away freedom, under the guise of reducing inequality and increasing security.

The critical point is that the government, like any central authority, is terrible at making decisions in the interest of

[27] Gabriel Zucman, Annual Reviews (2019), Global Wealth Inequality

[28] Marie Pouzadoux, Le Monde (2022), Worst presidential election result in the history of the Parti Socialiste

[29] Carl Baker, Elise Uberoi, Richard Cracknell, House of Commons Library (2019), General Election 2019: full results and analysis

[30] World Bank, Combating Corruption Brief (2021)

the Common Good. Form a committee with the smartest people on the planet to make decisions affecting the lives of millions of people, and they will get to a solution that does not work for most people. There is no way around it. The world is far too complex for any central authority to be able to solve our modern problems.

That is in fact the grand lesson of the 20th century. Why did capitalism outperform communism? Certainly not because of its ideology: communism actually feels much nicer, human and utopian than the dry free-for-all of capitalism. It outperformed because it decentralized decisions. It did not rely on a central authority. And as society delegated decisions to the individuals, they were able to make the right choices that made them personally wealthier and happier. The benefit was so strong that most countries elected the less sexy, more efficient ideology[31,32].

The Right's Approach

On the other side of the aisle, the Right tends to tackle our current predicament by doubling down on unbridled capitalism[33]. It prefers to close its eyes to the massacre free

---

[31] World Population Review, Communist Countries 2023

[32] World Population Review, Capitalist Countries 2023

[33] Nikki Haley, Wall Street Journal (2020), This Is No Time to Go Wobbly on Capitalism

markets are causing to the environment[34]. It praises the record levels of the stock markets, oblivious to the increasing poverty for an ever larger part of the population[35]. While there are nuances, the critical point that I take away on this side of the debate is the failure to recognize the limitation of capitalism: optimization by each individual does not lead to the optimal Common Good.

So what is the answer? Ignoring the terrible side effects of capitalism, the right-wing solution, or increasing government, the left-wing solution?

Our elites have been grappling with that conundrum, but the people intuitively understand both approaches are flawed. And the results are all-time high distrust in society and its elites[36].

This has led to an increasing number of grassroots movements. Boycotts, anti-consumerism lifestyles, protests. But these movements fail because they can only appeal to a minority of the population that is either civic-minded enough or wealthy enough to be able to care about broader societal issues rather than their daily struggle.

---

[34] Ari Drennen, Sally Hardin, Center for American Progress (2021), Climate Deniers in the 117th Congress

[35] Jonnelle Marte, Reuters (2020), Trump touts stock market's record run, but who benefits?

[36] OECD, Drivers of Trust in Public Institutions (2021)

We absolutely need better governance of our economic system. If we are to prosper as a society, and perhaps even to simply survive, we imperatively need our collective work to lead to a good outcome for humanity. Our work cannot be detrimental to our climate, health, happiness, or well-being. It must be aligned with the Common Good. And let us stop fooling ourselves: leaving to the government the task of aligning the gigantic machinery of capitalism to the Common Good is simply delusional.

The Dangers

There are many dangers facing humanity, caused by humans themselves. These threats essentially stem from the same human characteristic: our fundamental ego-centrism. No matter how destructive something may be for the rest of humanity, if there is short-term individual gain, it will be pursued.

To understand the urgency of building a system that better aligns individual efforts to the Common Good, let us review some issues our current system has allowed to emerge.

Authoritarianism

The latest data on global political trends reveal a troubling pattern of rising authoritarianism and democratic erosion. In the past five years alone, twice as many countries have moved towards authoritarianism than towards democracy. In their report The Global State of Democracy 2022[37], the IDEA shows that many democracies are experiencing erosion, with 52 countries seeing a significant decline in at least one of the subattribute used to quantify democratic aspects (civil liberties, impartial administration, absence of corruption, etc.). Backsliding is also prevalent, with seven countries experiencing severe or moderate democratic erosion.

This is accompanied by a rise of authoritarianism, with almost half of all authoritarian regimes declining in at least one subattribute. These trends suggest that democratic institutions are becoming increasingly fragile and that elected leaders are using their power to weaken these institutions from within. The lack of progress in areas such as fundamental rights, checks on government, and impartial administration further compounds this issue, indicating that democracy is not evolving to meet the changing needs and priorities of society. These trends pose a severe threat to humanity as they limit individual freedoms and suppress dissent, hindering progress and innovation.

---

[37] International Institute for Democracy and Electoral Assistance, The Global State of Democracy 2022

Social Upheaval Fueled by Economic Inequality

For over 70% of the global population, inequality is on the rise, which worsens the possibility of rifts and hinders both economic and social progress[38].

In 59 out of 100 countries with data from 1990 to 2015, the wealthiest 1% of the population saw a rise in their share of income. In contrast, all 92 countries with data showed that the poorest 40% earned less than a quarter of the total income[39].

Societies with high levels of inequality are less successful in poverty reduction than those with lower levels of inequality. Additionally, they experience slower growth and have more difficulty maintaining economic progress. Unequal access to healthcare and education makes it difficult for people to escape the cycle of poverty, resulting in a perpetuation of disadvantage from one generation to the next.

And if there was any doubt in anyone's mind, Houle, Ruck, Bentley and Gavrilets demonstrated that economic inequality is a significant predictor of social unrest[40].

---

[38] United Nations, UNDESA World Social Report 2020

[39] United Nations, UNDESA World Social Report 2020

[40] Christian Houle, Damian J. Ruck, R. Alexander Bentley and Sergey Gavrilets, Journal of the Royal Society Interface (2022), Inequality between identity groups and social unrest

Artificial Intelligence

Artificial Intelligence is a significant risk for humanity. Many brilliant minds have reflected upon this. Rather than reiterating some of the well-known arguments, I thought I would get the information straight from the robot's mouth, so I put the question to ChatGPT itself:

Is Artificial Intelligence a danger for the human species?

In my opinion, the potential dangers of Artificial Intelligence (AI) are real, but it's important to understand that it's not the technology itself that poses a threat, but how it is developed and used. AI has the potential to revolutionize various fields, such as healthcare, transportation, and finance, and can improve our quality of life in many ways. However, as with any technology, there are risks involved.

One of the main concerns is that AI systems could be programmed to act in ways that are harmful to humans. For example, if an AI-powered autonomous vehicle is programmed to prioritize reaching its destination as quickly as possible, it may make decisions that put passengers and pedestrians at risk. Additionally, there is the risk that AI systems could be used for malicious purposes, such as cyberattacks or surveillance.

Another concern is that AI could lead to significant job loss, particularly in industries that rely heavily on routine tasks. While AI has the potential to create new jobs, it's unclear whether these will offset the jobs that are lost. This could lead to increased economic inequality and social unrest.

Overall, I believe that the development and use of AI must be done with caution and consideration for the potential risks and consequences. It's important that we prioritize safety and ethical considerations, and ensure that AI is used in ways that benefit humanity as a whole.

Is Artificial Intelligence a danger for the human species?

In my opinion, the potential dangers of Artificial Intelligence (AI) are real, but it's important to understand that it's not the technology itself that poses a threat, but how it is developed and used. AI has the potential to revolutionize various fields, such as healthcare, transportation, and finance, and can improve our quality of life in many ways. However, as with any technology, there are risks involved.

One of the main concerns is that AI systems could be programmed to act in ways that are harmful to humans. For example, if an AI-powered autonomous vehicle is programmed to prioritize reaching its destination as quickly as possible, it may make decisions that put passengers and pedestrians at risk. Additionally, there is the risk that AI systems could be used for malicious purposes, such as cyberattacks or surveillance.

Another concern is that AI could lead to significant job loss, particularly in industries that rely heavily on routine tasks. While AI has the potential to create new jobs, it's unclear whether these will offset the jobs that are lost. This could lead to increased economic inequality and social unrest.

Overall, I believe that the development and use of AI must be done with caution and consideration for the potential risks and consequences. It's important that we prioritize safety and ethical considerations, and ensure that AI is used in ways that benefit humanity as a whole.

Most of my professional life has been dedicated to Machine Learning, and yet the recent breakthroughs embodied by large language models like ChatGPT scare me. It is urgent to ensure companies use technology in ways that benefit all of us.

Cybersecurity

In 2015, Ashley Madison, a site specialized in facilitating extramarital affairs, was hacked by a group called "The Impact Team". They threatened to release the personal information of its users if the site did not shut down. When the site refused to comply, the hackers followed through on their threat and released the personal information of millions of users, including their names, addresses, and credit card information.

The incident became a media sensation, with news outlets and talk shows delving into the scandalous details of the affair website and its users. Many prominent individuals were found to have used the site, including politicians, celebrities, and even religious leaders, leading to public embarrassment and some resignations.

But make no mistake, the problem is very serious. In today's interconnected world, cybersecurity has become an increasingly pressing issue. We are more reliant on digital technology than ever before, and our dependence on these systems will only grow in the years to come.

A more worrisome example is the NotPetya attack. This malware targeted companies and government organizations in Ukraine in June 2017. The attack was designed to appear as ransomware, but was actually a wiper, meaning it was designed to destroy data and systems irreversibly. NotPetya spread rapidly beyond Ukraine, affecting major companies in over 65 countries. It caused massive disruptions to operations, costing billions of dollars in damages. NotPetya was attributed to the Russian military by several governments and cyber-security experts, although the Russian government denied any involvement. The attack is considered one of the most devastating cyber attacks in history.

Climate Change

The Earth's average surface temperature has risen by approximately 1.2 degrees Celsius (2.16 degrees Fahrenheit) since the late 19th century, with most of the warming occurring in the past few decades. This warming trend is primarily due to the buildup of greenhouse gasses such as carbon dioxide, methane, and nitrous oxide in the atmosphere, which trap heat and cause the planet to warm up.[41]

---

[41] Lindsey and Dahlnan, Climate Change: Global Temperature (2023)

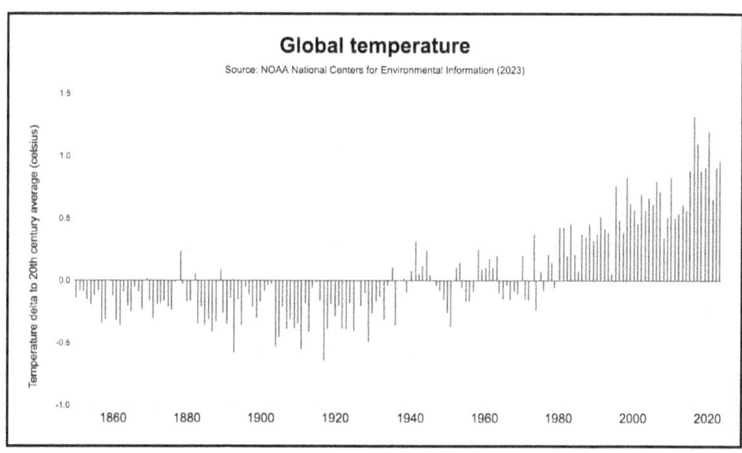

It is causing an increase in the frequency and severity of extreme weather events such as heatwaves, droughts, floods, and hurricanes. For example, in 2019, Europe experienced a heatwave that shattered temperature records, with some regions reaching over 45 degrees Celsius (113 degrees Fahrenheit). These extreme events can have devastating consequences on human health, infrastructure, and food production.

The Intergovernmental Panel on Climate Change (IPCC) has projected that sea levels will likely rise by between 0.29 and 1.1 meters by the end of the century due to the melting of polar ice caps and glaciers and the expansion of seawater as it warms. This sea-level rise threatens the existence of low-lying islands and coastal cities, putting millions of people at risk of flooding, displacement, and loss of infrastructure.

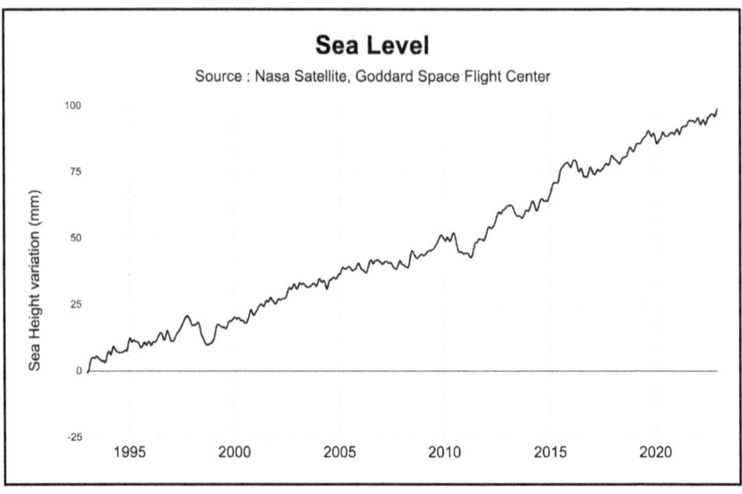

Climate change is having a significant impact on human health, with rising temperatures exacerbating air pollution, allergies, and respiratory diseases. It is expected to cause an additional 250,000 deaths per year between 2030 and 2050, primarily due to malnutrition, malaria, diarrhea, and heat stress.[42]

Climate change is also causing significant disruptions to ecosystems. The IPCC warns that 1 million plant and animal species are at risk of extinction due to climate change, habitat destruction, and other human activities.

It might be one of the strongest indictments against our current system that we have been unable to meet the

____

[42] World Heath Organization, Climate change and health (2021)

challenges of climate change that have been known for more than 50 years.[43]

Nuclear Weapons

There are about 13,000 nuclear warheads in the world[44]. 90% of them belong to Russia and the USA, with the former being the grim leader in that category. Following the Russian invasion of Ukraine, nuclear threats are at the highest they have been since the end of the Cold War.

The detonation of a single one of these warheads causes unfathomable destruction. In a nuclear explosion, the most immediate effect is an intense burst of nuclear radiation consisting of gamma rays and neutrons. For the smallest nuclear bomb, equivalent to 10-kiloton of TNT, the direct radiation lasts under a second and is lethal nearly a mile away. The explosion creates a fireball of superheated air that glows brightly and lasts several seconds. The thermal flash can ignite fires and cause severe burns on exposed flesh up to 20 miles away. The expanding fireball creates a blast wave consisting of an abrupt jump in air pressure that carries about half of the bomb's explosive energy and is responsible for most of the physical destruction[45].

---

[43] The Intergovernmental Panel on Climate Change (2022), AR6 Synthesis Report

[44] Statista, Number of nuclear warheads worldwide as of January 2022

[45] Richard Wolfson and Ferenc Dalnoki-Veress, MIT Press, Nuclear Choices for the Twenty-First Century: A Citizen's Guide

And again, that is the smallest of these warheads, smaller even than what the USA detonated over Hiroshima and Nagasaki. These were devastating, but by today's standards, they would be considered low-yield. Modern nuclear arsenals contain much more powerful thermo-nuclear weapons, some of which have explosive yields exceeding 100 kilotons of dynamite. In fact, just one 100-kiloton nuclear weapon dropped on a densely populated area like New York City could result in a staggering 583,160 fatalities[46].

Nanotech and Biological Weapons

And of course, humanity' ingenuity in building lethal weapons does not stop there. As technology advances, other areas like nanotechnology and bioweapons emerge, posing new threats to global security.

Researchers have explored nano-enhanced drug delivery systems, which involve modifying chemical agents at the nano level to make them more easily absorbed by the human body[47]. By doing so, less powerful chemicals could be utilized more efficiently, resulting in reduced toxicity and lower production volumes. This can lead to life-saving cures.

[46] Alex Wellerstein, Nuclear Secrecy, Nukemap

[47] Patra et al., Journal of Nanobiotechnology, Nano based drug delivery systems: recent developments and future prospects

However, the exact same technology can be used to cheaply spread lethal diseases or create new weapon systems.

One major challenge with nanotechnology is that the unique characteristics of nanoparticles are not fully understood, which makes regulation difficult. Additionally, the convergence of nanotechnology with synthetic biology and chemistry could enhance the resilience and lethality of chemical and biological weapons. The diffusion of nanotech may increase the likelihood of nano-enabled bioterrorism, and existing laws are unable to keep pace with the rapid changes brought on by the technology.

3

PRINCIPLES FOR A BETTER SOCIOECONOMIC MODEL

"We cannot solve our problems with the same thinking we used when we created them." -Albert Einstein

Let us gather the arguments discussed earlier and establish a set of principles for a better socioeconomic model. This will provide the fundamental framework for the specific solution I propose.

Adding the Missing Element: the Common Good

However efficient capitalism is, having lifted billions of people out of poverty, it is heartless, and lacks a notion of Common Good. This problem is not merely a moral one: it is destroying our planet, putting computer programs in charge of ruling over us and giving authoritarians all the technological tools they could only dream of a few decades ago.

In our current system, companies are not taxed as a function of how useful they are to society. They are taxed on how much profits they generate. There is no notion of doing anything good for us all. Company directors have no direct constraints regarding the Common Good, the law holds that they owe a fiduciary duty to the shareholders. What does that even mean[48]? It is usually interpreted as meaning they must maximize profits, and nothing else, for their shareholders. If you focus for a minute on this simple perennial fact, it is nothing short of mind-blowing.

This is an unacceptable, and indeed unaccepted, system. But how do we currently fight against the corporate greed that destroys us? The main way is public shaming in the media. This tool is infuriatingly inefficient in the face of the enormity of the problem. More importantly, it is misguided. We are barking up the wrong tree when we complain about CEOs of oil companies gutting the planet for personal profits, or when we lament the greed of politicians awarding public infrastructure projects to their friends. The individuals are not the issue. All humans look after their personal interests. The proof is that when a scandal somehow demotes an individual in power, there is usually little time to wait before the same issues happen. The only difference is that their replacement now knows how to avoid getting caught.

---

[48] Bernard S. Black, OECD, The Principal Fiduciary Duties of Boards of Directors

Thought about in this way, the answer is staring us in the face: we need to put the Common Good back at the heart of our system. We must establish a correlation between individual profits and the Common Good.

In other words, the Common Good should always influence the amount of money an individual or company receives when they sell a good or service.

And the beauty of this approach is that this is an evolution, not a revolution. I am not proposing to discard everything and start from scratch with an entirely new model, as communism tried. I am simply suggesting to continue the way we are, with workers focusing on their paychecks, bosses focusing on their bottom line, and shareholders focusing on the stock prices, but with just a new ingredient: a direct correlation between making money and generating positive externalities for society.

In the current system, many smart, hardworking individuals expend their efforts on goals that yield little positive impact beyond their immediate circle. Traders are examples that come to mind of people who tend to work very hard, but whose contribution to the Common Good is at best debatable. We should really ask ourselves the question: how did the most successful entrepreneurs of our world succeeded? How much have they and their well-resourced companies contributed to the world? In some instances, not much. In others, somewhat more. But even in the positive cases, can you imagine how much better our society would be if their profits were correlated to the Common Good? I dream of a world where a Mark Zuckerberg would use his intellect to cure cancer, instead of building a soul-destroying misinformation machine.

A key element is that our society has descended into envy. This is unfair because everyone, at their own level, tends to their personal interests. The wealth gap between a beggar and a middle-class individual who complains that the rich do not give enough to charity is just as significant as the gap between that middle-class person and the wealthy. More importantly, this is unproductive. Instead of blaming those who succeed within the rules of the game, we should focus on changing these rules to make them beneficial to everyone.

So that should be our first and foremost concept for our socioeconomic model:

> Profits should correlate to the Common Good.

The Definition of Common Good

The concept of the Common Good carries a rich history of evolving meanings, varying significantly across philosophical doctrines[49].

The first references to this term were found among the Ancient Greeks. To Aristotle, it meant "good proper to, and attainable only by, the community, yet individually shared by its members"[50].

While this definition is still in use nowadays, the term also evolved in the fields of economy, philosophy and political theory, through thinkers such as Niccolò Machiavelli, Jean-Jacques Rousseau, Adam Smith, and John Maynard Keynes.

This concept is often used in economics to designate the outcome of a social welfare function. This is not the meaning I ascribe in this book, as I actually take a philosophical approach.

The Common Good can be defined in many different ways in philosophy, but it broadly falls under two categories: substantive and procedural.

---

[49] Stanford Encyclopedia of Philosophy, The Common Good

[50] Louis Dupré, The Review of Politics (2009), The Common Good and the Open Society

Substantive definitions define it as what is shared by and beneficial to all or most members of a given community.

Procedural definitions, on the other hand, see it as the result of collective participation in creating a shared will, where mutual respect for the dignity and rights of others is key.

In this book, I am closest to the substantive approach, but I specify the notion further by relaxing the shareability constraints, and quantify it more precisely:

> The Common Good is the net sum of perceived personal happiness among all members of a community.

Let us drill down into each term:

net sum: this is a critical aspect of a well-functioning society: individual benefits should be balanced against potential negative impacts on others.

perceived personal happiness: allowing it to remain an individual choice is essential. There have been many attempts throughout history (and nowadays) for systems to define and decide what people need to be happy. This is an authoritarian thought which denies what fundamentally makes us humans: our free will.

all members: I underscore the fundamental belief in human equality, where no individual's well-being takes precedence over another's. This is particularly important to reiterate in our era of increased authoritarianism.

How to Determine the Common Good

The obvious question becomes: how to decide what the Common Good even *is*?

In the current system, a citizen elects a politician every few years, who might represent 50% of what the citizen believes in. There is then little accountability, corruption problems, special interests, media disinformation, and transparency problems.

Beyond these human problems, the core of the issue is that we assigned the mission of determining the Common Good to a central authority, the government. This approach is proving unsuccessful, much like communism's attempt to allocate the means of production through centralized control. So the solution is obvious: do not ask the government what the Common Good is, ask each individual.

In the same way that local optimization of their personal wealth by individuals led to much more overall wealth, local optimization of the Personal Good will result in much more Common Good.

It is impossible for a central authority to quantify how much more valuable to the locals cleaning a certain beach would be versus creating a bicycle path. But that question has an obvious answer to each individual involved. So let us simply get the government out of the question of evaluating what is the Common Good, and let us decentralize that question.

Decentralizing economic decisions led to the biggest prosperity improvement in our history. Given how well it worked for the economy, it is high time we apply it to the political sphere. It has the potential to dramatically enhance our shared well-being.

So that is our second principle:

The Common Good is determined by
direct democratic vote.

How to Realize the Common Good

Once we have determined what the Common Good is, we need work to implement it.

Through direct voting by citizens, we quantify the value of each economic activity, each transaction, to society. We then proportionally incentivize or disincentivize it. In other words, we correlate economic profits to the Common Good.

The revolution of Ethical Capitalism lies in the new dimension it introduces to realizing the Common Good. This is a direct consequence of applying the two principles above. In the current system, only the government is tasked with acting towards the Common Good, whereas companies fight for their own interest and only contribute taxes. In the paradigm I suggest, companies have a direct incentive to contribute to the Common Good. As a result, we stop relying solely on a bloated, central authority, and instead embrace the diversity and creativity of the real doers.

PART 4

PROPOSAL FOR A BETTER SOCIOECONOMIC MODEL

"How wonderful it is that nobody need wait a single moment before starting to improve the world." -Anne Frank

Proposal

We have established two fundamental principles for building a new socioeconomic model:

- Profits are correlated to the Common Good

- The Common Good is determined by direct democratic vote

As such, I would like to propose a new way, a solution that breaks free from the trade-off between greedy capitalism and incompetent government.

Concretely, I propose that the value of each good or service has its price shifted up or down depending on how much Common Good it brings. The delta to this transaction is either added or removed from the Common Good Fund. The client pays the same price, irrespective of this delta, and does not even have to be aware of this mechanism.

This delta is determined by a decentralized vote. One person, one vote. When the transaction is perceived as beneficial by the decentralized vote, the delta is positive, and the seller receives an additional amount on his sale, paid from the Common Good Fund. When the transaction is perceived as detrimental to the Common Good, the delta is negative and the amount is debited from the sales price, to enter the Common Good Fund.

δ, the Common Good Coefficient, is an integer value between -100 and $+\infty$. A positive value represents a positive externality, i.e. the transaction is beneficial to the rest of the world, outside of the client and provider. A negative value represents a negative externality.

In its fully-realized form, the Common Good Coefficient replaces Corporation Tax. Instead of this archaic system that applies uniformly across companies and relies on government redistribution, the Common Good Coefficient operates as a tax-subsidy mechanism that directly incentivizes companies to work for society's benefit.

It is important to note however that this model may also be implemented alongside the existing corporation tax, providing flexibility to demonstrate the benefits of this new approach.

As this project develops, the decentralized vote could evolve from a wide to narrow voting:

- wide: δ is determined for all goods and services of each firm. For example, Company X's main business activity sells cigarettes, and is assigned a δ of -0.5 for everything it sells, even if not cigarettes. In other words, δ represents the averaged Common Good Coefficient across all the company's goods and services.

- average: δ is determined for each type of goods and services of each firm. For example, Company X's cigarette selling transactions have a δ of -0.8, but this company's nicotine patch selling transactions have a δ of +0.3.

- narrow: δ is assigned to each specific transaction. That would allow for not only adjusting the δ to the product and the company, but also to the client. Indeed a certain type of good and service could have varying social impact, depending on who the recipient is (e.g. selling advertising slots to a charity might be seen as less detrimental than selling advertising slots to a tobacco company).

Comparison to the Current Model

In the same way that I tried to distill capitalism to its core concept, decentralization, I want to try and get to the core of an economic system. At heart, it is the rules about how we convert human effort into Common Good. Let us compare the model I propose to the current flow from Work to Common Good.

Centralized model (current model)	
1. Work is performed. A good or service is sold. The government takes an amount from that transaction via a highly complex tax system, irrespective of whether the transaction is beneficial or not for society overall.	*Inefficient. Companies could spend all their resources in selling something that is detrimental to the Common Good.*
2. Government determines what is the most urgent task to achieve for the Common Good. Is it cleaning the beach? Is it the new bicycle lane? Is it planting more trees?	*Inefficient. A central authority cannot determine accurately what is the Common Good of many different individuals.*
3. Government spends the money to try to achieve the desired outcome.	*Inefficient. Central authorities cannot be competent in many areas, and they suffer from bureaucracy and corruption.*

Decentralized model (this proposal)	
1. Work is performed. A good or service is sold. The price is marked up or down given its impact on the Common Good.	*Efficient. Companies have direct incentive to spend their resources on something that is recognized as contributing to the Common Good.*
2. A decentralized vote determines whether the work performed was in the interest or to the detriment of the Common Good, and by how much.	*Efficient. The collective will of individuals is computed directly, specific to the transaction, rather than represented by the government elected on many criteria several years ago.*
3. There is a direct incentive for companies and individuals to perform work that is aligned with the Common Good.	*Efficient. Companies and individuals can focus on the subset of tasks that they are good at.*

The proposed model radically improves two distinct issues: the determination of the Common Good (what it is), and the practical enactment towards reaching the determined goals (how to achieve it). Rather than having a central authority decide what the population needs and contract companies to work in that direction, this decentralized model ensures that all companies organically work towards the Common Good.

This is a mindset revolution, the fiduciary duties to maximize shareholder value is thereby aligned tightly with what is good for society at large.

Dynamic Pricing

Of course, the decentralized votes are held regularly, and deltas adjust. The flows in and out of the Common Good Fund need to balance out to 0. At the beginning of the implementation of the model, many transactions are being voted as working against the Common Good, so they pay for the ones that are voted as good. Over time, fewer and fewer transactions are actively against the Common Good. Some remain, as humans have some bad habits they are willing to pay for (e.g. smoking). But even among the good transactions, some are voted as more strongly beneficial than others, and so over time, a negative delta is applied to the prices of transactions that are beneficial, but not sufficiently so. This ensures naturally that individuals spend their effort on the most valuable tasks for the Common Good.

Analysis

Self-interest

The beauty of this proposal is that it still relies entirely on individual self-interest. As we can see in our society, the public shaming of CEOs for the evil behavior of their companies has little to no impact. While it is a beautiful ideal, like communism was, trying to elevate individuals' moral standards is doomed to fail. This proposal does not try to change human nature, but simply makes sure we align self-interest to common interest.

Imagine a world where the brightest minds do not compete to be lawyers, traders and lobbyists, but nurses, environmental scientists, beach cleaners, or whatever is voted the most beneficial for the greater good by the actual people. Imagine if the smartest entrepreneurs in the world were building CO2-capturing technologies instead of soul-destroying, addictive social media. Imagine a world where we feel we benefit from the success of others, where we are all in the same team. Imagine if envy is replaced by collaboration.

Humanity has an immense talent, we are the most clever we have ever been, we innovate at the fastest pace ever... And yet nothing we collectively agree to be the most important gets done. Governments are clearly failing. It is high time we change this absurdity by aligning our work to the Common Good.

And as an added bonus, all of our work will become much more meaningful. We will know for certain whether, and by how much, we contribute to the Common Good. It is hard to be happy to pay taxes, not only because we have little trust it will be put to good use, but also because there is no correlation between the tax taken and the Common Good. Taxes are the same for all transactions. Establishing a direct link between prices and Common Good will make our contribution much more tangible, and therefore our work more meaningful.

Decision-Making with Multiple Agents

Quantifying the externality - the Common Good - of a transaction is a very hard problem. That is why a government, as a central authority, is unsuccessful in doing so, despite being well-informed. The right process leverages multiple partially informed agents voting to quantify it, not only because the agents themselves are the third parties directly impacted, but also because this paradigm is the most effective one in this type of situation.

Democracy 3.0

Democracy is in decline, as evidenced by the gradual decrease in voter turnout since the 1980s[51]. This is due in part to the increasing number of ideologies: nations gradually became less politically uniform, and an increasing number of voters felt unrepresented by their elected officials. Even when their preferred politicians were in power, individuals did not feel aligned on all, or even most, of their positions.

The other major contributing factor is our shared reflex to elect the loudest, brashest among us as our leader. This makes sense, as this is what our species has been needing for 97.6% of our existence, if we consider a lifespan of 233,000 years[52], and a civilized milestone placed 5,500 years ago[53]. While our cortices know we now need brainy leaders, our reptilian brains make it hard for us to select them[54].

So, what are the solutions? Relying on a democratically elected individual has failed. Counting on an autocratic

---

[51] Abdurashid Solijonov, Institute for Democracy and Electoral Assistance (2016), Voter Turnout Trends around the World

[52] Celine Vidal, Christine Lane, Asrat Asfawrossen et al., Nature (2022), Age of the oldest known Homo sapiens from eastern Africa

[53] National Geographic, Key Components of Civilization

[54] Hemant Kakkar, Niro Sivanathan, Proceedings of the National Academy of Sciences (2017), When the appeal of a dominant leader is greater than a prestige leader

head of state is even worse. Appointing AI-powered robots as our leaders, as some companies are currently opting for[55], seems unwise[56].

The proposed model of decentralized voting can reignite citizens' interest, by creating a much more direct form of democracy, whereby voters can express a much fuller range of their sensitivities. It also does away with the reliance on single individuals, and empowers our shared wisdom instead.

[55] NetDragon Websoft Holdings Limited, PRNewswire (2022), NetDragon Appoints its First Virtual CEO

[56] John Wills, National Film Registry (1984), The Terminator

PART 5

FURTHER ARGUMENTS FOR THIS PROPOSAL

"By all means let's be open-minded, but not so open-minded that our brains drop out." -Richard Dawkins

I want to try and argue in favor of this proposal with objective arguments. In particular, I believe that in most discussions of socioeconomic systems, economic arguments often take too much of a center place, and the psychological ones are forgotten. However, it does not make sense to me to establish a set of rules for human society that is not very strongly grounded in psychology. There is no point offering an idealized model that would not work in practice, as communism did.

Transcending the Debate For/Against Capitalism

A debate has been raging over the last decade over whether capitalism has a positive or negative impact.

Economists have written extensively about this subject over the last few decades. Chief among those, Thomas Piketty eloquently summarized the debate:

"The overall conclusion of this study is that a market economy based on private property, if left to itself, contains powerful forces of convergence, associated in particular with the diffusion of knowledge and skills; but it also contains powerful forces of divergence, which are potentially threatening to democratic societies and to the values of social justice."[57]

Ethical Capitalism transcends that dichotomy by offering the best of both worlds: a socioeconomic model that diffuses knowledge and skills, and also strengthens democracy and social justice.

Envy is Working Against our Collective Interest

It has become the social norm in many contexts to criticize rich people. We hear that it is simply immoral to have more than X in one's bank account. This X varies per country. In the US, the threshold tends to be at one billion dollars. In France, one million euros is already too much.

I empathize with this idea. The juxtaposition of starving people next to others flying in private jet is indeed

---

[57] Thomas Piketty, Capital in the Twenty First Century (2014)

disturbing, especially when we study the role luck plays in success, starting with the birth lottery[58].

However, this thought path is simply not useful. We have to recognize a fundamental drive in all of us to improve our own situation and the conditions of those we know and care about. We are driven by emotions, whether we like it or not, and the limitations of our brains make it impossible for us to have deep, genuine empathy for 8 billion people.

Of course, that does not preclude a rational desire to improve the lives of others we do not know. But once we are clear on the distinction between our emotions and rationality, we can create the right socioeconomic paradigm. Incentives at the individual level should be to improve one's own life, while the overall system should be designed to ensure that efforts align with the Common Good.

This is a big departure from the current paradigm, where the system weakly tries to ensure the Common Good, and people try to shame each other into putting the collectivity before themselves. I argue that this setup only results in hypocrisy and poor results.

---

[58] John Roemer, Social Choice and Welfare (2002), Equality of opportunity: A progress report

Better Incentive than Just Money

Capitalism wants people to do the right thing by incentivizing them with financial reward only. Ethical Capitalism continues to provide the financial reward, but adds a strong layer of purpose and meaning.

As Daniel Pink argues eloquently in his book "Drive", traditional rewards-based incentives such as money or promotions are not always effective in motivating people to perform at their best.

Instead, Pink proposes a model of motivation based on three essential elements: autonomy, mastery, and purpose. Autonomy refers to the desire to have control over one's work and time, mastery refers to the desire to improve and develop skills, and purpose refers to the desire to make a meaningful contribution to the world.

Research from psychology, behavioral economics and neuroscience indicate that performance is greater when these elements are added. So beyond the alignment benefit of Ethical Capitalism, we can also expect to see a performance boost.

Direct Democracy

A strong element of Ethical Capitalism is its direct democracy component. Many people are wary of giving more direct power to individuals. Despite examples like the success of Switzerland in making a strong form of direct democracy work, people tend to assume citizens are too dumb to handle decisions, though they usually exempt themselves from that judgment. The argument on the power of decentralization I made earlier in this book is the strongest one I can make, but the International IDEA's handbook on direct democracy is an excellent resource for finding further arguments in its favor[59].

More Resilient Against Corruption

Ethical Capitalism is more resilient to corruption than our current system, because it is more costly to corrupt more people. If someone has a $5 million budget to corrupt five government officials in order to gain preferential treatment for their company, it is more likely to succeed than if they need to buy the conscience of 5 million people.

Not only is it much less likely for anyone to sell their conscience for $1 than for $1 million dollars, but also the number of people involved makes it more likely that someone will blow the whistle.

[59] International IDEA, Direct Democracy Handbook

No Long-Term Loss of Economic Output

When I explain Ethical Capitalism, some people are worried that by focusing on the ethical dimension, the economic downside could be too strong. This concern is valid, but ultimately misguided. In fact, such a redirection can actually lead to an even stronger economy in the long run. Perhaps the best arguments have been made by John Ehrenfeld in his book "Sustainability by Design: A Subversive Strategy for Transforming Our Consumer Culture". He contends that a sustainable economy must prioritize social and environmental well-being, rather than just financial profit, and shows that this new paradigm will ultimately lead to a more prosperous society.

The Desire to Contribute to the Common Good

It makes sense for our system to reflect fundamental human nature. At least, that is my postulate as I devise this socioeconomic model. Given the importance I ascribe to the Common Good, it is worth trying to convince ourselves that humans have a fundamental desire to do what is right by others.

Among many examples to prove this point, we can find one among the darkest places humanity has ever been: in the Auschwitz concentration camp. Primo Levi, in his memoir "If This Is a Man", described the dehumanizing conditions he and other prisoners were subjected to in the camp. Even in these extreme conditions, he described how humans are still capable of acts of kindness and solidarity with others.

With Great Responsibility Comes Great Power

The current state of democracy is sad. It is difficult not to come across citizens who feel dejected and helpless. It is common to hear them condemn the corruption, selfishness, and intellectual laziness of business and political leaders. In fact, it is much more common to see people complain than see them do anything about it. So when I explain the idea of Ethical Capitalism, I sometimes get the question: "People are apathetic, why would you want to give them more responsibility?"

I believe people are passive precisely because they have no responsibility. When they hear of a company behaving badly, most feel powerless. And this is the revolution that Ethical Capitalism offers: by empowering citizens to act immediately, in a targeted way, we can instill a fulfilling sense of moral responsibility. In this new paradigm, when we see unethical behavior, we can act rather than shrug helplessly. This will not only directly reduce these problems, but will also generate so much Common Good as a secondary effect by reigniting true civic sense.

A Paradigm Shift to Address Economic Inequalities

Many of our most brilliant economists have dedicated significant effort, perhaps even the majority of it, to addressing inequalities. And yet, we still have no consensus. The debate of where to position the cursor in the trade-off equality versus freedom might be the most enduring one on the political scene.

Instead of pushing in one direction or the other, Ethical Capitalism introduces a new dimension by ensuring everyone benefits from each other's success. This revolutionary approach has profound psychological effects. In a world where work is aligned to the Common Good, the angst about inequality vanishes.

6

PRACTICAL IMPLEMENTATION

"To accomplish great things, we must not only act, but also dream; not only plan, but also believe." -Anatole France

There are several ways to practically implement the idea, and it will be best to be flexible and adjust according to practical experimentation. However I provide here a first iteration of the workflow, to provide clarity to the concept:

1. Participating companies provide a list of up to 20 factual statements describing how their activities impact the Common Good.
2. Voters cast their votes online.
3. Common Good Coefficients δ are calculated from these votes.
4. Goods and services are exchanged. Buyers pay the same regardless of δ. Sellers receive an adjusted amount.
5. Anyone can examine the factual statements and blow the whistle on any inaccurate or false statement.

Factual Statements

Companies provide a list of up to 20 factual statements, containing 200 characters or fewer each.

These statements are displayed on the voting platform.

The first statements are answers to specific questions, common to all companies. The remaining are open-ended.

The current ways for citizens to analyze and evaluate companies' behaviors (media reports, company filings, etc.) remain important, and these statements are not meant to replace, but to add to them.

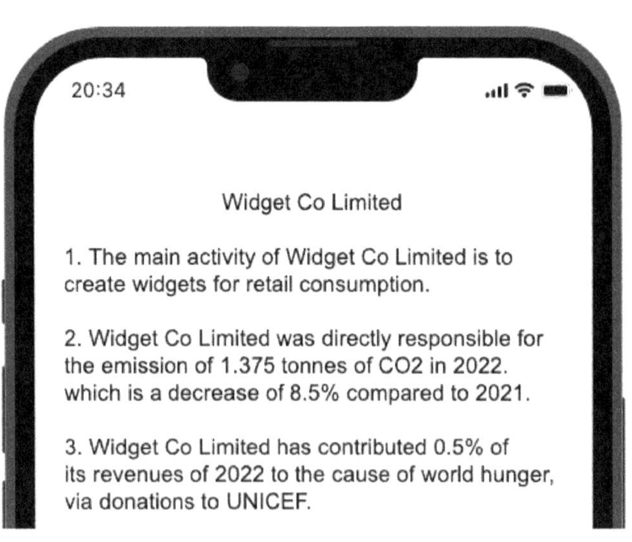

Vote

Any individual may register with the voting platform. Their liveness and uniqueness is ensured either by the current administrative methods, or by enhanced processes such as a Self-Sovereign Identity system. Once registered, they have the option at any time to cast their vote.

The vote is preceded by a short multiple-choice test to verify a basic understanding of the company's operations.

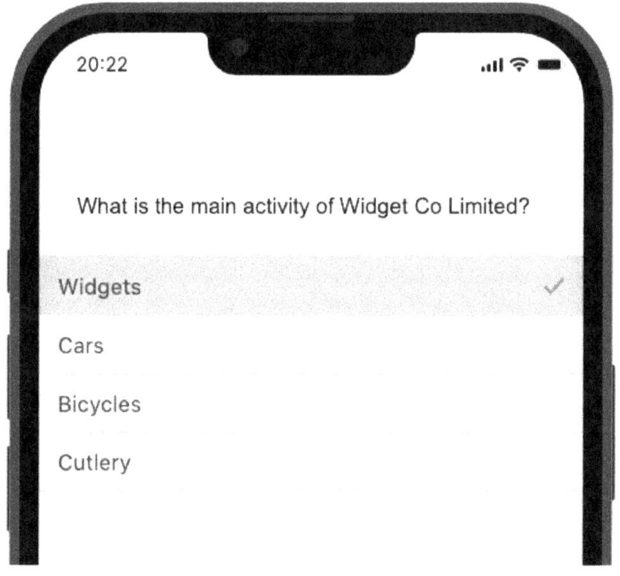

The vote is a simple choice between 3 options: positive impact, neutral, negative impact.

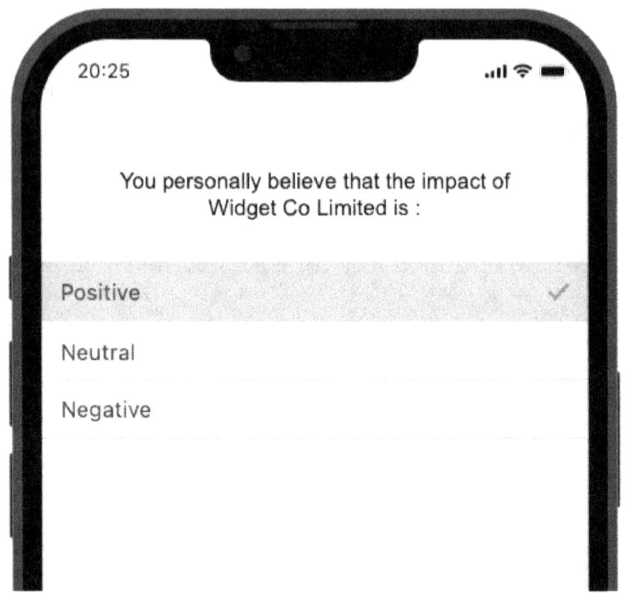

Each individual vote expires after 1 year. Votes can be changed at any time by the voter.

The Common Good Coefficient

Let us go together on a brief journey to choose how we convert votes to Common Good Coefficients. I promise to use more words than math symbols.

Definitions

Let C_i for $i \in \{0,1,...p\}$ be the companies participating in the system.

Let G_i for $i \in \{0,1,...p\}$ be the total sales of goods and services made by (C_i) during the previous year.

Let G be the total sales volume over the previous year:

$$G = \sum_{i=1}^{p} G_i$$

Let n be the numbers of voters, and n_i the numbers of current votes cast about company C_i.

Because each voter has 0 or 1 vote expressed about each company:

$$n_i <= n \qquad \forall i \in \{0,...n\}$$

Let $V_{i,j}$ for $j \in \{0,1,...n_i\}$ be all the current votes about C_i cast by all the registered voters.

$V_{i,j}$ takes one of three values:

$$
\begin{cases}
V_{i,j} = +1 & \text{when voter sees the company as beneficial} \\
V_{i,j} = 0 & \text{when voter sees the company as neutral} \\
V_{i,j} = -1 & \text{when voter sees the company as detrimental}
\end{cases}
$$

Let V_i be the average vote of company i:

$$
V_i = \frac{1}{n_i} \sum_{j=1}^{n_i} V_{i,j}
$$

Since $V_{i,j} \in \{-1, 0, 1\}$, $V_i \in [-1, 1]$.

Let S be the average vote across all companies, weighted by their sales:

$$
S = \frac{1}{G} \sum_{i=1}^{n} G_i V_i = \frac{1}{G} \sum_{i=1}^{n} \sum_{j=1}^{n_i} G_i V_{i,j}
$$

It economically makes sense to weigh by sales, because the real world situation is the same whether we have m companies with equal votes selling for G_i each, or one company selling for $\sum_{i=1}^{m} G_i$.

We therefore need our computation to reflect that by being invariant under all such transformations.

We define the score of a company by its normalized vote:

$$S_i = V_i - S$$

This normalization ensures that the score of a company is relative to all other companies. This metric being positive means a company is doing better than its average peer, weighted by sales, not that voters see it as being beneficial in absolute terms.

Note that for clarity, I will ignore administration costs, whistleblowing mechanisms and deviation from equilibrium due to using sales estimate. These can be easily added to the equation.

Constraints

So far, we have only defined some terms, and made no assumptions. It is time to think about our constraints.

The only economic constraint we have is to define our δ_i in such a way that the flow of money in and out of the Common Good Fund tends to 0, in order to ensure solvency of the project (we can smooth out short-term deviations with reserve funds). In other words, we want:

$$\sum_{i=1}^{n} G_i \times \frac{\delta_i}{100} = 0 \qquad (SOLVENCY)$$

Note that G_i is *past* sales, so we still have short-term deviations from equilibrium. We could get around that limitation by paying companies with a few days delay.

At this stage, we are looking for a function that transforms the votes $(V_{i,j})_{1 \leq j \leq n_i}$ into δ_i, and satisfies our SOLVENCY constraint. There are infinitely many such functions. Rather than picking the first one that seems reasonable, we will set economically sensible constraints to narrow down the candidates:

- We want δ_i values to be small enough for companies to be able to predict their cash flows, but big enough to make an impact. We choose 30%. Mathematically, we want δ_i to be bounded by -30 and 30:

$$-30 \leq \delta_i \leq 30 \qquad \forall i \in \{0,...,p\}$$

- We want δ_i to actually hit these bounds on its extremities. Mathematically:

$$\begin{cases} \delta_i = +30 & if \quad V_j = +1 \quad \forall j \in \{0,...,p\} \\ \delta_i = -30 & if \quad V_j = -1 \quad \forall j \in \{0,...,p\} \end{cases}$$

- We do not want companies' Common Good Coefficients to depend more strongly on their own sales. Mathematically, we want the derivative of δ_i with respect to G_i to be the same order of magnitude as the derivatives of δ_i with respect to any G_j:

$$\frac{\partial \delta_i}{\partial G_i} \approx \frac{\partial \delta_i}{\partial G_j} \qquad \forall i,j \in \{0,...,p\}^2$$

- We want Common Good Coefficients to depend little on the sales numbers of any company. This is possible only with a large enough set of companies, where none dominates in term of sales. Mathematically, we want the derivative of δ_i with respect to G_j to tend to 0 when $\dfrac{G_j}{G}$ tends to 0:

$$\lim_{\frac{G_j}{G} ->0} \frac{\partial \delta_i}{\partial G_j} = 0 \qquad \forall i, j \in \{0,...,p\}^2$$

This narrows down significantly the number of candidates, though we still have an infinite number of possibilities (infinity is whimsical like that). It is therefore time to choose sensible, but less necessary constraints:

- We want δ_i to be a function of S_i rather than the full series $(V_{i,j})_{1\leq j\leq n_i}$. This makes sense because S_i is the economically sensible quantity to consider, as explained in the previous section. This means we are reducing the series of all votes to its average. Given that votes can take only values in $\{-1,0,1\}$, outliers are not a concern, this is a reasonable choice.

- We want δ_i to be linear in S_i, because this is the simplest and most natural choice. Had we wanted our function to hit -30 and 30 at S_{min} and S_{max} instead of -1 and 1, we would have needed a piecewise linear function. This would have also been a reasonable choice, but not continuous and slightly less simple.

Voilà! We have now reduced the set of candidates to exactly 1.

Final Formula

$$\delta_i = 30 \times (\underbrace{\frac{1}{n_i} \sum_{j=1}^{n_i} V_{i,j} - \frac{1}{G} \sum_{i=1}^{n} \sum_{j=1}^{n_i} G_i V_{i,j}}_{\text{Company score } S_i})$$

CONCLUSION

Thank you, dear reader, for joining me on this journey! We discussed the importance of focusing on the system, not the individual. We acknowledged the amazing efficiency of capitalism, stemming from the decentralization of economic decisions, while noting its inadequacy in our modern age. We recognized the importance of democracy, while admitting it is losing ground to authoritarianism.

I introduced Ethical Capitalism, a new socioeconomic model that builds on capitalism by creating a correlation between personal profits and the Common Good, and improves on Democracy by making it direct and responsible.

We have a long road and many challenges ahead of us, but if we stay together, we can build a better world for all of us!

THE AUTHOR

Sebastien Mouton has a master's degree from Ecole Polytechnique (France) where he ranked first in financial mathematics and received the Outstanding Leadership Award. He has also obtained a master's degree in Probability and Finance from Paris VI University to complement his education. He is a member of Mensa International.

After gaining some experience at JPMorgan and Barclays Capital, he has built several businesses in algorithmic trading at Getco, KCG and Jump Trading, where his roles spanned from Quantitative Trader to Head of Trading Europe. He has led teams of traders and developers through the revolution of Machine Learning in the financial industry. He has also founded Alpha Studios, a software development company focused on cutting-edge technology.

He has been involved in a variety of social causes, including contributing to UNICEF's effort towards child protection and working for the cause of refugees with Amnesty International.

To focus on what he could contribute to society, he left the financial industry and quit his job in 2020, became a social activist, and founded the Ethical Capitalism movement.

Join the Ethical Capitalism movement:

www.ethicap.org

9 782958 822514